Presented To

_____

From

_____

Date

_____

Making Your Life in the Outdoors

Making Your Life in the Outdoors

*Finding Meaning in the Crosshairs, and
Memories at the end of Your Line*

G. Warren Elliott

Drawbaugh Publishing Group
444 Allen Drive
Chambersburg, PA 17202

We thank Mariah Hertz for preparing the illustrations used throughout this book.

ISBN 978-0-9892680-2-8

For Worldwide Distribution, Printed in the United States.

1 2 3 4 5 6 7 8 9 10 / 17 16 15 14 13

Contents

A View of Life

All of us need our own special places to sit, a place to
reflect on our day,
The successes we had, or what we hope to forget.

It's crucial to find one or two, but some never do,
Though the results are immediate and therapeutic for you.

I found mine when I was fifty or so;
Places to sit, to do nothing; places to where I love to go.

I've watched people in towns, on a porch, in a chair.
I drive by, they pause, and they look, and they stare.

They're looking for something, something not yet
around;
I believe it's their soul's place they seek, but have not
yet found.

Now the view can be varied, not always Thoreau;
More important is the tranquility of the place that
you go.

Instant peace, sublime calm, and serenity in that space;
Shielded from life's problems, concerns, and today's
hectic pace.

I task you to find it or them, as the case may be;
A glacier in Alaska, by a river, and a cabin view work
for me.

But find it you must, for your life to be complete.
Find your view, find your spot, sit down, take a seat.

Breathe in life's good air, and exhale life's tolls;
Ingest God's good grace, and stabilize your soul.

You'll be glad that you did; get away from your strife.
Sit down, take a look, and find a view for your life.

Introduction

Life is Full of Lessons

Life is full of lessons. They present themselves to us each and every day, yet they can be hard for us to grasp. I have found that I need one of several ingredients present for me to be able to connect with those things that are meaningful in the pursuit of growing and maturing as a human being.

Simply put, for me, the ingredients are family, friends, food, fishing, and forests. When any of these are involved, so too am I. The events that occur when these elements are present in my life often take on a meaning deeper than is immediately apparent.

The stories contained in this book were written in and around my five "f's" as I have named them. Wonderful times on the water or in the woods where special things have happened that have changed my life—life lessons, if you will.

This book is being published after I lost my two very best friends within four months. Greg was fifty-five and succumbed to pancreatic cancer; Terry was sixty and had a heart attack.

Making Your Life in the Outdoors

The impact of their untimely deaths on me has been profound. Yet, I am optimistic, and I want to encourage others to seek the opportunities of special times, special places, and special people so they, too, can remain positive in the face of tragedy. As Dr. Seuss says, let's "not cry for the loss, but be glad for the smiles that you had."

As you read my stories and enjoy my recipes, I encourage you to find what is meaningful to you and embrace it. Seek your special places to learn life's lessons, and go to them often.

Chapter 1

Reflections in the Woods

Making your own way in the outdoors may just make finding your path in life easier.

Buck! Buck!

Some "city slickers" did occasionally come to Archie's Cabin, including Archie's son, Tony. Tony had never shot a rabbit or a squirrel or a pheasant, let alone a deer. Tony was a golfer, not a hunter, and he was a best friend of mine. He was also the son of our cabin's founder, Archie, and I knew that it was important to Archie to have Tony there with us—in fact, it was the reason I was there.

So I kept Tony coming to camp by keeping him happy and making his life easy, oh so easy! I cleaned and oiled his gun, and picked out and kicked out his place to hunt. Heck, I even bought his license for him each year.

And while he wasn't much for hunting, he did like to eat. He especially enjoyed my cooking—all of it, even hog maw. But I digress, back to hunting.

Making Your Life in the Outdoors

It was a very cold first Monday of hunting that year. The wood stove had struggled all night to keep the cabin at shirt-sleeve temperatures. My alarm went off at five, and I could immediately feel the cold on my nose—but it felt good! The first morning always meant bacon, home fries, and eggs in the basket for breakfast. That all takes awhile to prepare, and we liked to head out to the woods by 6:30—our stands were really close—so get up I must.

The fire was almost out, so I scraped the remaining coals forward to place some kindling on them as I stoked her up. The outside temperature read 17 degrees, and it was only 52 inside. I got breakfast ready as the country music station forecast a cold and windy day. Predictably, Tony and Archie were the last to get out of bed and come to the table.

Even without cold weather, it was tough to get Tony to hunt. And now at 17 degrees, well this would take all of my persuasive skills. I reminded Tony the deer pot was now up over $200—an impressive amount considering that it grew annually by about $40. Or depending on how one looked at it, it could be considered depressing given that it had been five years since anyone had shot a buck from our camp.

"You have to shoot a buck to win that pot." Tony bemoaned. "I've never even shot my gun!"

"Ah, but this is your year," I told him convincingly, except for the fact that I told him the same thing every year. "Just go out there for a little bit this morning…this is the best time," I said to encourage him. He agreed to go on one condition—he would take his pillow and his sleeping bag with him to "stay warm."

And so it went. Tony was the picture of hunting fashion in his fluorescent orange flap hat, with bibbed pants to match, the snap waist of which no longer came close to clasping shut across his now expanded waistline. Gun, pillow, and sleeping bag in tow, off he went to his already prepared spot down by Sadler's cabin. It was a good spot, too, a downed tree along a small spring that never went dry. Tony was to crouch down in the fork of the tree and rest his gun on a branch for a surer shot.

As for me, I always sat at the same spot, 120 yards up the hill above the cabin. I usually sat still too, that is, unless I got too cold. And on this day the chill got to me by 10:30, so I walked down and joined Archie who was "road hunting," walking up and down the driveway.

"You seen Tony?" I whispered. Just as Archie was about to reply, fourteen deer, including several nice bucks, crossed the road below us and headed directly toward Tony's stand.

We waited for the shots to ring out. This was indeed Tony's year.

Then…then…nothing.

What was he waiting for? Archie grew impatient. Suddenly, impulsively, Archie yelled at this son. "Tony! Buck! Buck!"

As we came to learn later, Tony heard Archie's call and awoke from his snuggled forest slumber surrounded by deer, his gun resting alone on the forked branch several feet away.

No, Tony didn't get a shot that day. In fact, he never took a shot all the years he hunted at Archie's cabin. He did, however, eat hog maw for the very first time that evening, but that, as they say, is another story!

Life 101

The woods are incredible, soul-nourishing, and stable.
I get there often, as time permits, and when able,
To escape to a place and a time of life past;
To cling to it, to cherish it, and hope it will last.
Away from deadlines, goals, sales, and commissions,
Where one acts and reacts, on survival, not permissions,
Of keeping the heat, the food, and stacked wood,
Of stoking the fire and cooking meals that are good.
Life need not be complex, but can be what we choose,

'Cause when you cherish very little, you have little to
    lose.

So cut one more log or shoot one more deer,

Fill up your life freezer, set goals that are clear.

Set your heart on a course without man's imposition.

Trust your inner most instincts, make your own
    disposition,

Of what matters and doesn't, what's meaningful and
    counts,

Versus numbers and revenues, and "goods" that will
    mount.

Live life, live long, live happy, live free

Live joyfully, live simple, live you and live me.

Old Reds and Tony's Diapers

Old Reds hunted at the same place every year, below Sadler's camp (the next camp below Archie's), by the old fallen log by the spring. He would arrive every year at 6:15 in the morning on the first day of buck season in his 1977 Chrysler sedan. He parked in Sadler's driveway and was generally the only person to hunt at that camp. He usually did pretty well, as the deer had a trail that followed the run that emanated from the spring and ran right up to where Old Reds sat.

But Reds was getting older, slower, and weaker, and little did we know that 1985 was to be his last year hunting. That was also the year Tony would become a father, and he was hunting down toward Old Reds's stand that year.

Well, Reds shot a deer and shortly thereafter saw Tony walking the trail. Tony had heard the shots and came to investigate.

Reds was glad to see Tony as he had a deal for him—$10 to gut his deer for him.

As we know, Tony had never shot a deer let alone field dressed one, so he was not in his element to say the least. But what came out of Tony's mouth as an answer to Reds's request was one of the most memorable lines I ever heard at deer camp. Tony's response, and I quote, "I get sick changing my own baby's diaper…there's no way I could do that!" he said, looking at the deer.

Reds cleaned what was to be his last deer, Tony helped him put it in the trunk of his car, and we never saw Reds again. Tony did, however, get better at changing a diaper.

"People Let Me Tell You about My Best Hunting Friend"

When I think about my friends, I have been blessed in life to have some very special ones. Young, old, male, female—I could not describe my typical friend except to say that they are unique, interesting folks who, for whatever reason, care a lot about me.

Most of them, as my wife is fond of saying, are "colorful individuals." This means that they often march to the beat of their own drum, so to speak. I seem to attract and connect with these often quirky, different people—good people—no, great people!

But there is one friend who has stood head and shoulders above the rest—Greg Hertz, my best friend since the seventh grade. We have done everything together. We double-dated, we rode motorcycles, we grew our hair long, we partied, we lived together, we shared the sorrows of losing loved ones, and we have hunted together at Archie's Cabin for over a quarter of a century.

No one could ask for a better friend. Greg is unassuming, unpretentious, generous, and trustworthy. Yes, trustworthy beyond belief. In fact, I have often commented that if I were sent to the bottom of a deep well pit, and the only way out was to climb a rope held by only one person. Greg would be the only person I would want on the other end of that rope.

He has always been there for me, even though we live hours apart. When I ran for public office, he supported me although he lives outside the voting district. When I was selected as a Penn State Mont Alto Centennial Alumnus, he came to the ceremony. Of his many good traits, Greg is reliable.

So with that history in mind, as I write this he has for the first time in my life, shaken me. He has just told me that he has been diagnosed with cancerous tumors in his pancreas and his liver, and I know that it is my turn to be there for him. Fifty-five in my mind is a young age to be faced with such an overwhelming malady. In fact, just last year at hunting camp he was finishing years of schooling to become a professional engineer. The classes were rigorous, and many times he believed that his stomach problems were due to nerves related to the classes and tests that he was required to take, rather than the cancer that was sneaking into his body. I admired his determination, and his setting such a lofty goal at this stage in his life. I'm sure his classes were filled with kids half his age or less.

But he persisted, many years missing a day of hunting or an evening cabin meal due to his class schedule. When he wasn't at Archie's, it wasn't the same. I rely on his steadiness, I enjoy his company, and hunting season isn't hunting season without Greg's presence.

I try not to think of the prospect of Greg not being with me at Archie's in the future. Right now, we must get him better, whether for one or one hundred more hunting seasons. You see, a friend like Greg only comes along once in a lifetime, and that is only if you are very lucky.

The times that we have had in the woods are among the very best. We have never even shot a deer together. Doesn't matter. Just sitting at my deer stand talking about families, old times, good times, was so special.

I don't love many people, but I love Greg. Some say like a brother, I say even more so because there is no "blood" as the basis for our relationship. It started from scratch, and for forty-two years it has grown stronger and deeper every year, just because of the person he is.

I admire Greg. There will never be another person like him. He is my best friend ever, and for the record, he has always been a much better hunter!

Good luck, Greg!

Note: Greg Hertz passed away on August 1, 2009, five months after this story was written.

Old Dogs and Men *Can* Learn New Tricks— Like Cooking!

A woman's work is never done.
Lots of chores are just no fun.

Reflections in the Woods

Men prefer tasks that begin and complete,
Like waxing the car or hunting for meat.
No one cleans house or does dishes for yucks,
And doing the laundry…quite frankly, it sucks!
So be kind to your girlfriend, your lady, your wife;
She's probably better than you, and with care,
Will last your whole life.
Offer to help, come on, get a clue,
And pick up after yourself,
It's the least you can do!
My hunting and fishing buddies,
Well, they do cause me strife;
They leave messes, can't cook or clean,
And I'm not even their wife!
So think about changing as you read this whole book,
You'll be surprised at your home life,
If you just learn to cook!

Recipes

Grilled Venison Filet with Blue Cheese and French Onions

Ingredients

Extra Virgin Olive Oil (EVOO)
Chopped garlic
1 venison filet 1½" thick
Crumbled Blue Cheese
1 can French's Fried Onions

Sweet corn, peeled and cleaned
Fresh tomatoes
Fresh Mozzarella cheese
Vinaigrette dressing

Instructions

Marinate filet in EVOO, chopped garlic, salt, and pepper for one half hour. Boil water for corn and turn on grill to high. Add corn to boiling water and boil 8-10 minutes. Place filet on hot grill, cooking 3 minutes each side for rare. After flipping twice, place Blue Cheese on filet and cover to melt cheese. Place filet on plate and sprinkle with the fried onions.

Serve with the sweet corn, and sliced tomatoes with mozzarella cheese drizzled with vinaigrette.

Sauer Ribs—a great way to start the New Year

Menu

Sauer Ribs
Mashed Potatoes
Canned or frozen Sweet Corn
Hot Rolls/Bread and Butter

Ingredients

1 bag of sauerkraut
1 jar of applesauce

Reflections in the Woods

½ cup brown sugar
2 slabs of baby back ribs

Instructions

Grill ribs until just browned. Combine the other ingredients. Place ribs in a slow cooker and cover with the mixture. Set cooker on high until boiling; then turn to low and cook an additional 4 hours.

Roasted Southwest Pheasant

Menu

Pheasant
Corn on the Cob
Crusty Hot Rolls
Butter
Salad with Vinaigrette and Crumbled
Blue Cheese

Ingredients

Pheasant parts cleaned
1 quart buttermilk
1 egg
Southwest Spice Mix
Fresh corn on the cob
Butter
Bag of fresh rolls

Making Your Life in the Outdoors

Bagged spring mix salad
Vinaigrette dressing
Container of crumbled blue cheese

Instructions

Place pheasant parts in a zip lock bag with buttermilk. Put bag in a bowl or pan and place in refrigerator for a minimum of two hours. Preheat oven to 375 degrees. When fully marinated, remove pheasant parts from frig. Beat the egg and dip the pheasant parts in it. Roll in the spice mix to fully coat. Place parts on a wire rack in broiler pan and top each with a pat of butter. Place pan in preheated oven and cook for 50 minutes.

In the meantime, bring a pot of water to boil for the corn. Do not place corn in boiling water until pheasant is done. While pheasant is cooking and water is coming to a boil for the corn, place salad in bowls, dress, and sprinkle with crumbled blue cheese.

When pheasant is done, remove from oven and place on oven-proof platter and cover meat with foil. Pour juices from the pan into a saucepan, add ½ cup of water and bring to a boil; then pour au jus into gravy pot to serve with the pheasant. Place corn in boiling water for 6 minutes or place on plate with 2 tablespoons of water, cover with plastic wrap, and microwave on high for 10 minutes. Place rolls in 375 degree oven for 5 minutes.

When corn is done, uncover meat and serve with gravy. A tasty meal and so much easier than it will appear to your guests!

Pork Roast a la Maw/Hog Maw—a dish featuring tender pork, healthy vegetables, and a backwoods taste.

Menu
Roast Pork a la Maw or Hog Maw
Fresh Applesauce
Hot Crusty Bread or Biscuits

Ingredients
2 pounds pork loin
Extra Virgin Olive Oil (EVOO)
Flour
6 golden thin-skinned potatoes cut into bite-sized chunks, skin on
½ cup sliced green onions
2 cups chopped cabbage
½ cup asparagus tips

Instructions

Cover pork loin in flour, salt, and pepper. Heat EVOO in frying pan and sear the pork loin until golden brown all over. Mix the vegetables.

Making Your Life in the Outdoors

Place the browned roast in a baking dish. Surround the roast with the vegetables, salt and pepper to taste, and add ½ cup water. Cover the pan and bake at 350 degrees for two hours.

*An alternative and more traditional recipe for hog maw:

Ingredients

1 pig's stomach, cleaned (available at
butcher shop or grocery store)
¼ head of cabbage
2 russet potatoes
1 pound loose country sausage
(no fennel or Italian sausage)
½ small onion
Salt and pepper to taste, less is better

Instructions

Dice potatoes, cabbage, and onion. Mix with sausage, salt, and pepper and stuff stomach with the mixture. Use fondue sticks, wood or metal, to close stomach. Place on a rack in a roasting pan, salt and pepper outside of stomach. Put ½ cup water in bottom of pan, cover, and bake at 350 degrees for 3 hours. Uncover last ½ hour to brown skin. Slice and serve with ketchup.

Liver Pâté on Crackers—don't knock it till you've tried it!

Ingredients

1 pound chicken livers
1 hard-boiled egg
Good mustard
Mayonnaise
Sliced green onion
Worcestershire sauce
Salt and pepper

Instructions

Sauté the chicken livers in hot butter until no longer pink inside. Chop the egg and the green onion.

Place the livers in a small mixing bowl and mash with a fork until a fine consistency. This can also be made in a food processor.

Add a small amount of mustard and mayonnaise and Worcestershire sauce and mix thoroughly to form a paste, adding more mustard and mayo as necessary. Add the chopped egg and onion and fold into the pâté. Salt and pepper to taste.

Press the pate down into a bowl and cover the pâté itself with a piece of plastic wrap. Then cover the bowl and refrigerate for at least two hours.

Serve with good crackers; I suggest Triscuits or Wheat Thins.

Venison Steak with Fajita Marinade

Ingredients

2 tablespoons McCormick Fajita Marinade
2 tablespoons vinegar
2 tablespoons Extra Virgin Olive Oil
1 tablespoon lemon juice
1 venison steak ¾" thick

Instructions

Mix the first four ingredients in a small bowl. Place liquid mix in a zip lock bag and add steak, turning to cover. Place bag on a plate and refrigerate for 4-6 hours, turning over once. Preheat grill to medium then grill steak 4 minutes per side for medium rare. Discard marinade.

Venison Spaghetti Sauce

Menu

Venison Spaghetti
Tossed Salad (available in a bag at any grocery store) with Italian Dressing
Texas Toast or Garlic Bread (both in the frozen foods section of the grocery store)
Glass of Wine (Chianti or Merlot goes well with this menu)
Beer- A cold Coors or Straub is always good as well

Reflections in the Woods

Ingredients

1 jar DelGrosso Spaghetti Sauce
2 tomatoes
6 large mushrooms
1 chopped green onion including the stalk
½ teaspoons garlic salt
2 pounds ground venison burger
Spaghetti
1 teaspoon butter
1 teaspoon Extra Virgin Olive Oil (EVOO)

Instructions

Chop tomatoes, onions, and mushrooms into a chunky mixture. Heat EVOO and butter in a medium frying pan over medium heat until melted and just bubbling. Sauté the vegetable mixture in the butter and EVOO until soft but not browned or overcooked.

Pour the sauce into a saucepan and add the sautéed vegetable mixture. Put the sauce on low heat.

In the same frying pan, add a bit more EVOO and brown the venison, adding the garlic salt and breaking the venison apart as it cooks. It is okay to start it while frozen. When the venison is nicely browned, dump it into the sauce and simmer on low for one hour, stirring often but not constantly.

After the sauce has been simmering for about 45 minutes, cook desired amount of spaghetti according to directions on box. Drain spaghetti and serve in a large bowl with venison sauce over the top. Grated parmesan cheese is a nice addition to the spaghetti.

Chapter 2

Reflections in the Water

Fishing, like life, is a mystery—you never know what you will catch.

Take a Kid to Fish

Hins Pond is not much bigger than an Olympic size swimming pool. It has generally steep banks and access for fishing from a primitive dock built by Joe Hins, a farmer who uses the platform that rises ten feet above the water to "feed" the fish. Joe feeds his fish all sorts of things: stale cereal; dead groundhogs that unceremoniously pay their dues by becoming infested with maggots that ultimately drop into the water as food; and, yes, occasionally even some real fish food. Needless to say, in the heat of the summer this is not always the most pleasant of places to be. But it does have fish, big fish, and lots of them. And they are usually easy to catch.

Both my sons learned to fish at Hins Pond. So, too, did some of my friends' sons. It was a good place to go for success, which is exactly what you need to get a kid interested in fishing. Children have many attributes; however, patience is not among them. So it was good to have a place where we could "guarantee" success, regardless of the time of day, year (we even ice-fished the pond), or the type of bait or lure used. Just cast out and you would probably catch a fish.

Have you ever watched a child catch his or her first fish? It is amazing fun to look into the child's eyes as he or she winds the line, feeling the steady pulling but not knowing what is there. Then listen to the yelps of excitement! "I got one, I got one!"

Once landed, some children will want to touch their catch. Others will have a disdain and not want to do anything but look at it—it's all good! And they will want to catch another. This is an ideal time to begin to extol the virtues of catch and release, or how to properly handle and humanely kill and bleed the fish to make it best for the table.

Consider your equipment when you go. A basic push-button reel is a good start. Show them how to cast, and use bobbers to make their first bites easy to detect. Go a little heavy on the line as they will tend to yank the rods and wind harder than necessary to land their prize.

Early and quick success is critical to gain their interest in this sport. Don't let the fact that they are not yet embracing the techniques that take time and dedication to acquire on their initial outings.

Also don't forget the food and snacks. Kids love to eat.

Pack a picnic lunch. Let them help plan the menu. My kids always wanted a PBJ, peanut butter and jelly sandwich. Take a break when things get slow, or it gets too hot, or just to eat. Bring lawn chairs and congratulate them on their catch. Don't—I repeat, don't—out-fish them even though you can. You are important enough in their eyes and don't need to prove a thing except…that you love them.

"Let's Go Fishing!"

Dad's hat, sunglasses, fishing box, and pole;
We headed to the pond, me and my excited five-year-old.
These were big adventures, with mysteries to marvel;
Even though it was just a farm pond to which we would
    travel.

He was doing Dad's thing, just as Dad did,
And that made it special, for both Dad and his kid.
The box contained lures, quite frankly a mess,
But they were his and his alone, to be used for success.

Dad tied on a bobber, and a small plastic grub,
Which he threw in the pond, and hoped for a tug.
Be it sunny, or catfish, or perhaps a bass would take
    hold,
He wanted to be like me, the mighty fisherman, so big
    and so bold.

A proud moment for Dad, a special moment in life,
Simple times, simple goals, without conflict or strife.
Just a bobber, the water, my son, and best wishes
For his tomorrows, for his happiness, and a life full of
    fishes.

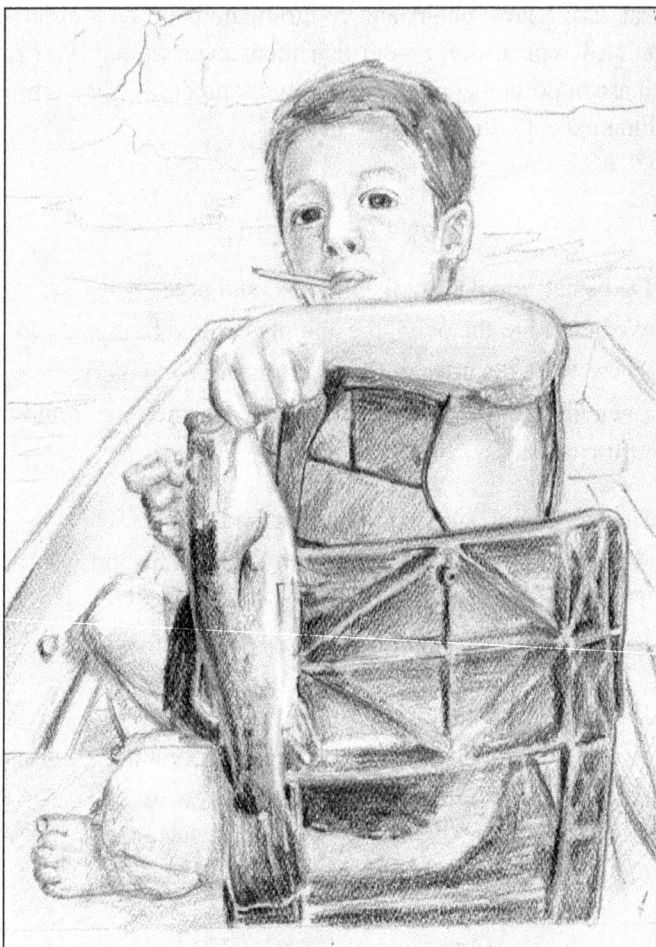

How I miss those days; yes, they went by so fast.
I knew it at the time, but still thought they would last
For more than a moment, a blink of the eye.
And as I look back at the pictures, they still make
    me cry.

I miss those special times, I miss my little guy
Who's now out on his own, no longer my small fry.
I walk to pond's edge, no pole, no retrieve;
Just casting for memories that get tougher to believe.

Time is a thief, stealing parts from each book and each
    page
Of our memories, our thoughts, as each of us age,
Of those times oh so special, so easy, so great,
They leave us so quickly, I guess that's our fate.

But better to have done, and then to forget,
Than never to have done, and live to regret.
I'm glad I have pictures, they rejuvenate my mind;
It makes aging less evil, makes memories less blind.

Here he comes once again, with smiles and wishin'
"Get out of the chair, Dad! Please take me fishin'!"

Dying for a Drink

It was a Friday evening, Memorial Day weekend, 2007. It was quiet at the River House, our weekend waterfront getaway cottage. The Juniata was flowing at a low-level for this time of the year and there was not a hint of wind.

I was alone and decided to take the boat out and go fishing. I had a 17' Grumman with a jet motor—ideal for a river whose Indian namesake means "Standing Stone." My boat ramp had just been reconstructed the previous October and this was only the second time I had used it. As I unloaded the boat into the water I noticed a couple swimming about 150 yards upriver in front of the "drug house." The "drug house" was the last place up our lane and it looked like a bunker—all basement, no house on top. Whether there ever was a structure on top of the concrete block foundation is subject to debate. Some said there once was a house there; others suggest the basement was all that ever got built before the owner ran out of money. In any event, everyone on the river was aware of the place and its nickname. Cars came and went at all hours of the night; they didn't stay long, either.

But there they were—two people swimming, laughing, and yelling. One was a male and one a female. The female was a heavyset blonde, seemingly the same person I had just met a week earlier when I knocked on the door as I went up and down the dirt road to see if anyone would help me repair the pothole-filled lane providing access to our cottages. I was determined to ask everyone to help, yes, even the folks at the "drug house." At the least, I thought they might have a little extra cash and that their "clientele" would appreciate the road improvements!

The blonde was the one who had answered the door and, well, she was less than appreciative of my organizing this little fund-raiser. Her father, whom we had heard was dying of cancer, lie snoring on the couch. It was an uncomfortable visit at best; but the fact that I now knew her would soon become significant.

In any event, I got into my boat and began to head down-river. There was no wind, and I soon decided to just drift with the current. I shut off my motor and cast toward the shore looking for my favorite fish, the small mouth bass. By 7 o'clock I had drifted a half mile and had not caught one single fish. I was about ready to head upstream when the heavyset blonde, whom I had seen swimming earlier and who was still wet, yelled at me from the shore. I could not understand her, and she began to leave.

I put the trolling motor down into the water and headed her way. As I did, I came upon something that had been following me down the river as I drifted along fishing. As I always do, I wanted to get this apparent piece of trash out of my river, so I swung wide, grabbed it, and approached the girl who had now stopped, seeing that I was coming to talk to her. What I scooped out of the river was a half empty bottle of cheap whiskey that I placed on the floor of the boat.

"I couldn't hear you," I said to the girl.

She asked, "Have you seen a guy swimming in a black t-shirt and a black and white hat? His name is Tim."

"No," I responded, and then said, "I know you, don't I? You live at the end of the lane," now recognizing the less than enthusiastic blonde who had greeted me at the "drug house" last week.

"Yes, I do," she said. "My friend and I were swimming, but now he's missing," she added.

At this point I noticed that she had no shoes on and said, "I saw you swimming. Did you walk all this way here in your bare feet?" I was intrigued that this pale, overweight young woman could be three-quarters of a mile downstream in wet shorts and with no foot protection.

"No, my mom is in a van up on the road. She drove me here to look for Tim," she responded.

Again, I told her that I had not seen anyone, but would go look for him, at which point she headed away from the stream and back to the pothole-filled road.

There was only one other fisherman on the water this night, so I shouted at him and asked him if I could talk to him. He reluctantly trolled over toward me, as I did to him. We met in the middle of the river and I introduced myself and explained that a young man named Tim was missing and that I was going to go upriver to look for him. I asked if he would join me. He told me his name was Steve and he agreed to help. We decided that I would patrol the west shore and he would search the east.

As he started his motor, I spotted something floating in the water. It was small, much smaller than a man, but was black and white and I asked my fellow fisherman about it. He said it was a dead duck, perhaps a Canadian goose based on its colors, that had been floating there for some time, perhaps a half hour or so. As he got ready to leave, I told him that I wanted to go look at it. I had never seen a dead Canadian goose in the river, and was curious about its apparent fate. As I trolled closer, I began to see the outstretched arms and legs that hung down below the water line from what I soon realized was not a goose but a black and white foam hat.

Yes, it was Tim, and I yelled for Steve to come and help me. He motored to me and we turned the body over to see if we could revive him—all to no avail. Water gurgled from his mouth and nose and his skin was blue, his eyes open, listless, and dark. Oddly, his stare reminded me of the videos I had seen of a shark…lifeless and ominous. It was all unsettling and eerie.

I immediately used my cell phone to call the police. I first reached 911 Perry County Dispatch who put me through to the Newport State Police Station.

"I have a drowning victim here in the Juniata River," I told them.

"What is your name?" came the response, "and where are you?" I answered both questions and then received a directive to stay where I was and not to touch anything.

"Too late," I said. "We are drifting down the Juniata River, and we already turned the body over."

"Stay where you are and we will come to you," said the voice from the police station.

"Do you have a boat?" I asked, "Because I can see the Amity Hall boat ramp from where I am. We can meet you there in five minutes." It seemed to be the most expedient thing to do. After a short debate, the state police relented and said they would meet us at the ramp.

It was decided that we would load the body onto Steve's boat because it sat a little lower in the water. I would proceed to the ramp and ask the people there to leave so as not to startle or upset anyone—we had nothing with which to cover the body.

I got to the ramp and everyone cooperated and left. At the same time, many of the locals, who were listening to police monitors, descended on us. It turns out that my accomplice, now docked with the body on board, worked for the state police in their computer department and was recognized by some of the officers as they arrived.

As to what happened next...well the next three hours are somewhat of a blur. Bits and pieces of what happened are as follows:

I tell the state police that I have a lot of information and can shorten the process for them. They ask me my name, address, and Social Security Number. I answer their questions as they begin to check me out. Then once again I tell them again that I have information that will help.

"What is it that you know?" they finally ask.

I respond by telling them that I know his first name— "Tim"—that I know where he was swimming, who he was with, and where she can be found. I also give them the bottle of whiskey and intuitively tell them that I think it might be evidence, admitting though that I had touched it in case they checked it for fingerprints.

Well, for the next three hours or so I tell my story to the state policeman, then the investigator, then the Deputy County Coroner. The area is cordoned off in fluorescent orange tape and the TV cameras arrive. Steve and I are separated, and I am "locked" in a patrol car. I am given a yellow tablet and pen and instructed to now write everything as I remember it in great detail and then to sign my "sworn" statement. I do so. So, I learn later, does Steve.

By eleven, we are "released." It is pitch black, and I am not looking forward to running my boat upstream one and a half miles to the cottage. I am even less looking forward to being by myself. Tim's image is already haunting me. The lead investigator asks me if I'm okay, or if I need counseling. I thank him but say, "No." I ask the state police if I will hear from them. They tell me, "Only if necessary." I ask them for business cards and they respond that they don't have any, but proceed to write their phone numbers on a piece of torn yellow tablet paper and give them to me.

Steve loaded his boat and I said good-bye to him. I headed up the river in darkness trying to remember where the rock outcrops were so I could avoid hitting them. Everything happened so fast. I went from being alone, to being surrounded by people, to being alone again.

I got back to the River House in time to see two unmarked police cars heading back toward the "drug house." They were there until midnight. For me, I called my wife, I prayed, I called a special friend, and I prayed some more. It was hard to get to sleep that night. Other than the day my mother died and an occasional funeral, I had never been exposed to a corpse before and had certainly never ever found one.

41

I began to think about this day. I wondered, *Why me? Why was this part of God's plan?* Perhaps it was one more lesson about how precious life is, what a gift it is. Perhaps I needed to be there so this young man's family and friends didn't wait anxiously for days, or weeks, not knowing Tim's fate as his body washed farther down the Susquehanna River. At least they had closure, and I had provided it.

Whatever the reason, the experience changed my life forever. I learned much later that Tim's body was full of drugs and alcohol. And the last his blonde friend had seen him was when he was chasing that bottle of whiskey that had drifted away from them down the river. A river that was only three feet deep at the time. *What a shame,* I thought. *All he had to do was stand up. Instead, he truly did "die for a drink."*

I couldn't eat that night!

Ice Fishing Done Warm and Easy

I don't like to be cold. When I hunt for whitetail deer in Pennsylvania in November and December I wear an insulated suit, extra socks, long underwear, lots of wool, and use plenty of hand-warmers. So, at first glance, the idea of ice fishing wasn't all that appealing. You may feel the same way.

But as with any other sport, there are ways to do it and be comfortable. I have ice fished now for fifteen years in temperatures as low as -5 degrees with a wind chill of -20 degrees. Admittedly, those were extreme and certainly not ideal conditions.

But, like anything else outdoors, if you prepare properly, (a friend of mine likes to say that "there is no such thing as bad weather, just bad gear") you can fill the slow time in winter catching some of the most delicious fish you will ever taste. My all-time favorite fish is walleye through the ice. The flesh is firmer, it appears whiter, and has almost no fishy taste or smell due to their low metabolic rate and feeding habits when ice is on the lake and the water temps are low.

And for the record I do mean *lake!* I have not, and will not, ice fish on streams. The currents are too unpredictable, and the varying structure and water depths make stream and river ice fishing too dangerous for me. I strongly advise against it.

Lakes and ponds, however, are a different story. Personally, although they say 2" of good ice will support a human being, I like a minimum of 4". Why take a chance? I start close to shore drilling pilot holes, and gradually work my way out to the deeper waters once good ice is found.

You will find that it's fun to "walk on water." You can get to all the good spots that are unavailable from the bank, or hard to hold from a boat in warmer weather.

We make a day of it. A small portable propane grill, frying pan, ketchup, and spatula are always in my bag. These are used to cook venison burgers on the ice. The smell of hot food, the taste of hot food, on the ice on a cold day is incredible.

Getting back to clothes, obviously, dress warm. I wear 2000-gram thinsulate boots with a polypropene "wick" sock, topped by a thick wool sock. Silk long underwear is topped by a set of Under Armor long underwear—expensive, yes, but well worth the money. Then I add a turtle neck shirt, a wool shirt, a neck and hood fleece, and my insulated bib overalls. I wear Walls Water-Pruf.

I top my outfit with a set of fluorescent orange ice spikes around my neck and a pair of ice cleats on my boots. No matter what the conditions, never go on ice without cleats!

To dig the holes in the ice, either a hand auger or a power auger will work. You will want a Vexilar Sonar; and I like my Fish Trap Pro ice shanty as well. Some jigging rods—I prefer 24" Frabills with a very light line, 2-4 pound test, will do the trick. Small jigs like the mamuska tipped with wax worms will

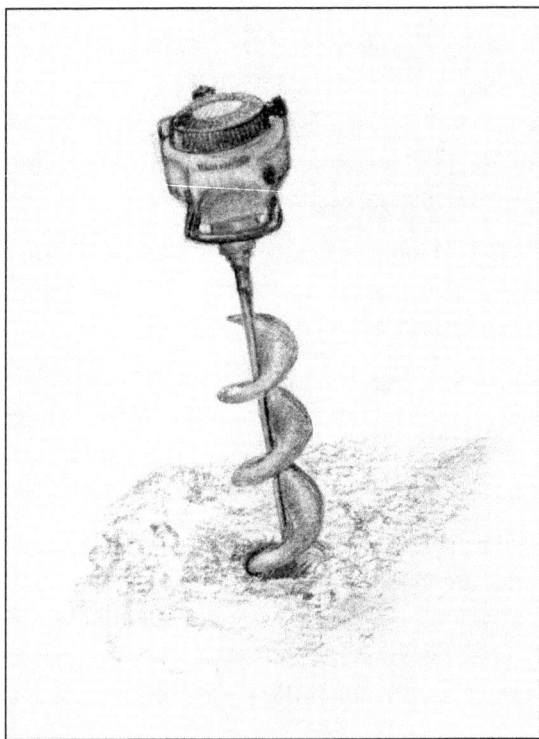

get you started. You will need to fish one to two feet off the bottom for success with most pan fish.

I will tell you the only time I keep or eat a bluegill, crappie, or perch is when they are caught through the ice. Like the walleye, the meat is firmer and fresher tasting. My whole family loves it when I bring them home.

Finally, consider this fact—no boat motors, no waves, few if any other folks fishing. Ice fishing while it is snowing is supreme—quiet, calm, beautiful solitude.

It's very easy to get started. An auger, rod, lures, bait, and a bucket to sit on can be had for less than $100. Wear your deer hunting clothes to begin. The Vexilar will cost you more but can be used on soft water as well.

It is time well spent when not much else is going on in the sporting world, and the meals that you will be able to prepare are unmatched.

Recipes

A New Fisherman's Picnic
Most important—let kids help plan!

Menu

PBJ (Peanut Butter and Jelly sandwiches), trim
crusts and cut into four squares
Fruit Juice
Potato Chips
Fruit—Apples, Bananas

Making Your Life in the Outdoors

Cookies
Soda, fruit juice and water

This is not a difficult menu. The most important part is letting the kids help plan and prepare the picnic. Let them choose the sandwiches and extras. Make this their day!

Bacon, Eggs, and Home Fries

Menu
Country-cured Bacon
Eggs in a Basket
Orange Juice
Fresh Strawberry Jam

Eggs in a Basket—a traditional favorite the kids love too!

Ingredients
Sliced bread, one or two slices per person
Brown eggs
Butter at room temperature
Salt and pepper to taste
Juice glass

Instructions

Butter both sides of each slice of bread. Press juice glass into the center of each slice to cut out an approximate 2″ round hole. Heat oiled pan or griddle to medium. Put bread in hot pan and break one egg into the hole in the center of each slice. Use a fork to occasionally distribute the egg white to ensure doneness. Add salt and pepper. Flip and cook to taste. Cook the center rounds cut from the slices in the skillet for dipping into the finished eggs or for jelly toast.

Home-Fried Potatoes

Here are two ways to make these:

1. Using leftover baked potatoes, slice them as thinly as possible and fry in a medium hot skillet in melted butter until brown. Season with salt and pepper.

2. Using fresh potatoes, slice thinly with a knife or use a hand slicer such as one found on a rectangular cheese grater. Heat butter in a skillet to medium high without browning it and add potatoes in layers. Add small slices of butter to each layer and season with salt and pepper.

Cover the skillet securely and fry for about 15 minutes. Then turn potatoes to brown the bottom and leave skillet uncovered. Potatoes are done when brown and softened.

Summer-Iced Walleye

Ingredients

1 lb. walleye fillets (perch, crappie, or bluegills can be substituted)
1 cup flour
Salt and pepper to taste
¾ cup Extra Virgin Olive Oil (EVOO)
1 whole fresh lemon
½ cup milk
Note: never let walleye fillets get warm or stand in their own liquid! Pat dry this and all fish before cooking.

Instructions

Cut walleye into 3" pieces. Dip in milk and roll in flour mixture seasoned with salt and pepper. My preference is less salt and more pepper.

Heat oil in frying pan until a drop of water sizzles when dropped in the oil. Cook walleye until golden brown. Do not overcook.

Reflections in the Water

Remember, guys, do not to use a metal spatula or tongs in your wife's non-stick (Teflon) pan! In fact, I prefer a cast iron pan.

Drain on a plate covered with a couple layers of paper towels and cover each layer with towels as cooked.

Serve with fresh sweet corn (10 minutes in boiling water) and fresh sliced tomatoes drizzled with balsamic vinegar. Place slices of fresh lemon in a bowl and squeeze lemon over fish to taste. (Can also be served with ketchup or tartar sauce.)

Chapter 3

Reflections through Another's Eyes

Helping others find their way
often helps you find your way.

Zack and the Fish Man

He seemed strangely out of place in the section of the creek we were fishing that day. We were several miles up Elk Creek, so it was rare to see anyone, let alone a boy, say, ten or eleven years old, seemingly by himself. His waders were old and ill-fitting—an adult size that came up and gathered under his arms. His rod was part spinning, part fly rod—a composite of pieces that he was either given or found in all likelihood.

He wasn't catching any fish either by the looks of it, but he was working hard at it. He was working his line, much like the rod suggested, sometimes casting, sometimes like a fly line. My guess was he was just mimicking what he had seen fishermen do on this stream, and was trying anything he could think of to get one of the finicky steelheads to bite.

Needless to say, our guide, known as Fish Man and quick to engage anyone he meets on a stream, struck up a conversation with the boy. His name was Zack, and his mother had dropped him off at the Girard Borough Park to fish for the day. Well, it was now almost 3 o'clock in the afternoon and the park was several miles away upstream. The boy was rough, almost crude. He laced his comments with the profanities that we felt he probably heard at home. Fish Man immediately called him on it, and told him in no uncertain terms to "knock it off."

"Why the hell should I?" the boy retorted.

"Because you sound stupid talking like that, and if you don't, I'm done talking with you!" Fish Man responded.

That seemed to get the boy's attention. Besides, Fish Man stands about 6'4" tall and must have seemed like a giant to young Zack. "I'm trying to catch a steelhead...never got one before," Zack said.

"Let me see your rod," Fish Man said, and he immediately went to work on it. He added some leader, put some split shot on, and tied on a lure much better suited to the conditions than what Zack had been using. Then he proceeded to show the boy where the fish were and how to cast. Within minutes, Zack called out, "Fish Man! I got one!" He fought the mighty steelhead successfully as Fish Man coached him through it, and eventually landed the boy's fish in his net.

"Now what?" Fish Man inquired of Zack.

"I want to take it home to show my mom and eat it," Zack said. Well, Fish Man usually prefers to return the beautiful trophies back to the stream unharmed, but he doesn't mind killing a fish if it is killed quickly and put to good use on a table.

Suffice it to say, we had our doubts the fish would ever be a meal. However, it was his first steelhead, and Zack was brimming with pride that would no doubt carryover when he would show his mom his catch. Fish Man briefly talked to Zack about catch and release for any future fish as he quickly broke the fish's neck and bled it out for the boy.

At this point, he told Zack that he should start home as we proceeded even farther downstream. Zack responded by heading back to the park where his mom was to pick him up, pleased, with his catch in one hand, the rod in the other.

I was once again impressed with the Fish Man, and felt good about fishing with him. We "lost" about an hour of fishing time being with Zack, but realized that it was a small price to pay, for Zack may have gained a lifetime of lessons from Fish Man's simple intervention.

When we left the stream that day, I reflected on the young boy with no apparent father to take him fishing, and identified with the feeling, as I had lost my own father at the age of five. But we didn't head straight home. Instead, Fish Man took a detour, back toward the park until he found a local police officer whom he hailed. He proceeded to tell the officer of the boy on the stream, and asked the officer to go to the park and check on him and to be on the lookout for his mother.

That was the right thing to do. It was 7 PM, and the world was good. Thank you, Fish Man.

Bright Eyes and Braces

As first published in PA Angler and Boater Magazine

If I laughed at him, he simply wouldn't go. But my tall, thin, 14-year-old son was simply a sight to behold in Dad's waders and wading shoes that required three layers of extra thick socks to even get them close to fitting. His small frame inside the neoprenes resembled a swizzle stick in a cocktail glass, as if he could have spun entirely around without touching the fabric. But I mustn't chuckle, or even call attention to his attire. He wasn't that excited about this trip to Erie for some early spring steelhead fishing anyway.

Now he did get a day off from school. But the cool weather and overcast conditions had dimmed his enthusiasm. The clunky shoes and the excessive volume of his clothes only further suggested that Mrs. Gibbon's English class wasn't looking so bad right now.

So I was quiet as we walked across the parking lot to our guide Fish Man's suite at the El Patio Motel. Fish Man is an affable and knowledgeable friend of mine with whom I have fished for many years. Things quickly got better as we entered the room that was a veritable Mecca of all things steelhead.

In fact, the room smelled of the famous "eggs" that Fish Man used to increase his hook-up ratio. There were rods and hats and photo albums and egg sacks and lures and flies almost everywhere. All we needed was some water and some fish and we could have just stayed there!

Fish Man immediately sensed the reluctance of a teenage boy to be in Erie in an uncomfortable outfit on a cold day and went right at him.

> *I once asked Fish Man to tell me about his secret eggs. He asked me point-blank if I could "keep a secret." I assured him that I could. His answer was a courteous but curt, "So can I." And that is the last time the subject ever came up.*

"Hey Logan, we're going to get you your first steelhead today," he promised. "In fact, I think that you will out-fish your dad today," he added to Logan's increased attentiveness.

Logan liked the idea of a guarantee to catch a fish. Better yet, to catch more fish than his father sounded good, too. Fortunately, I knew that these were not hollow promises, but rather that Fish Man would deliver. First, I have never, ever, gone fishless with this masterful guide of the Erie water system. And second, if Fish Man devoted his fish-catching prowess to Logan instead of me, then guess what—in all likelihood, I probably would be out-fished!

During the drive to Walnut Creek, and then as we walked into the stream, Fish Man continued to draw my son into his world of loving the outdoors. The stories flowed as easily from the Fish Man as any Lake Erie tributary does after the spring thaw. And Logan was buying them—hook, line, and sinker.

They had connected, and Logan had long ago forgotten about the clumsiness of his outfit, now laden with a poncho as the drizzle started, as he landed his first Erie steelhead. Not one to smile profusely, all I could see were braces and bright eyes as he proudly displayed the soon-to-be released fish for me to capture on film.

And so went the day, fish after fish, all successfully put back into the cold creek unharmed, a fact that I would learn later was especially meaningful to Logan. To his credit, Fish Man also took the time to explain to Logan the various rock structures and compositions that could be seen on the 100' high walls along the stream. The two of them also spent time fossil hunting, finding remnants of what once were delicate plant leaves now permanently engraved on the shale stones.

Fish Man has an innate ability to teach. He connects with people, and young folks take immediately to his educated, but easygoing style. My son was no exception, and it was heartening to watch. From each fish caught and released, to each stone turned over, wisdom about nature, about life, was being transferred in a manner few experience. What a way to learn! What a great day! It was so much fun to fish with my son, even if, or especially because, I was out-fished. Now, how did I write that "educational-day-off" memo to the school officials?

Bob's Burger

Sometimes in life you meet people just for a moment who can impact your life forever. Presumably, many of us have had a schoolteacher who would fall into that category. But here, I'm talking about an encounter in just an everyday moment of short duration but nonetheless, dramatic.

For example, when I bought the cottage on the Juniata River—I call it the River House—the boat launch ramp was in a terrible state of repair. The concrete had shattered under the pressure of water and ice over the years, and large chunks were either lifted or missing altogether. It was useless.

On the main road out of Duncannon on the way to the River House, I had seen a homemade sign advertising "concrete work" and a phone number. Previously I had stopped in to see a local contractor with a legitimate office but got no response to my needs. So I took a chance and met the individual behind the sign, his name was Ken.

Ken was local, living just a few miles above my place. He struck me as "good people" and we settled on a price to redo the ramp in its entirety.

To complete the job, Ken needed to enlist the services of a backhoe. His brother, Bob, had just such a piece of equipment and would come on-site to assist in the construction. It is Bob about whom I write in this story.

Bob was in his 60s and had been around equipment, farming, and construction all of his life. When I met him, I could tell immediately that he worked hard from the chafe of his hand in mine as he shook hello. He was lanky, quiet, and all business. He was also adept at operating a large piece of equipment. As the project began, I watched him work. He could use the huge bucket on the front almost like an extension of his hands. It was, in a word, graceful.

He could reach out and seemingly pick up a single stone at a time or one specific shovel full of dirt as the diesel engine revved and billowed clouds of smoke. He was good at what he did—an artist—and I liked him.

The ramp was completed, and a year later I needed my driveway and the road leading to my place repaired. The stones on the road were long gone, and the drive back was a slow and tedious trip due to the mud and potholes that had developed. I called Bob and enlisted his help.

He visited me and gave me a price. It was a fair price, and I authorized the work. Bob did the rest. Using his dump truck and backhoe, he set to the task, once again displaying his marvelous skill at gently operating these huge machines. Midway through the project, he advised me there was a way that he could finish the job better, and at a lower cost than the one he had proposed. I agreed, and he made the road and driveway like new.

When presented with the bill, I rewarded Bob with more than he had asked for. He was obviously pleased but both unapologetic and comfortable with accepting the inflated payment, which was still under his original quote.

Days later, Bob and his wife came back to see me. He thanked me for my generosity and gave me some meat from a steer he had just butchered. I learned later that Bob did not like to feel indebted to anyone, and the meat was his way of thanking me and, once again, gaining the upper hand in our relationship.

The road held up real well but Bob did not. A year and a half later at a meeting with local officials, I learned that Bob had succumbed to cancer and had passed away about a year after I last saw him. This troubled me. I would have liked to have seen him again. Although not knowing him well, I missed him and people like him. Skilled craftsmen who could "do it all," who were unassuming, and although un-educated, had more intellect and common sense than many in today's world can claim. It seemed that Bob's type were leaving us.

On Sunday, after hearing about Bob on Tuesday, I called his brother, Ken. I found out that Bob, filled with cancer, chose to shoot himself rather than suffer the inevitable pain and indignity. Most importantly, he wanted to avoid becoming a burden on his family and friends as he spent his final days on Earth.

Ken told me the story of Bob's final hours of life. He was so appreciative of my phone call during which I offered not only my condolences but also the story of the respect that I had for his brother.

Afterward, it bothered me that we consider ourselves to be such a humane society, yet it seems that we can be more humane to animals than to our own kind. I don't know Bob's faith, or his convictions, but obviously he was comfortable with his decision. I think he took a brave and perhaps admirable action. I do not and cannot question his decision to end his life. However, I do wonder if we could have made the decision easier, more honorable, and more comfortable for him in a physical sense.

Bob was a good man and the hamburger he gave me was delicious. Thank you, Bob, and God bless you.

Wally's Best Day

As published in PA Angler and Boater Magazine

Wally was in his middle 70s. A simple man of modest means, Wally had been a factory worker in Kane, Pennsylvania, for most of his life. He was devoted to Joanne, his wife of many years.

Wally wears funky hats, his glasses are a little thick and often crooked, and he has a broad, infectious smile, full of large teeth. A frozen hip causes a bit of a limp in his walk.

Now I generally get along with folks from Wally's generation and Wally is no exception. Like most people born in the 1920s and '30s, Wally knows what it is like to live through tough times. As a result, he is prudent, conservative, and no-nonsense. He is from the "old school" where the wife does all the household duties, so I never ask Wally to help cook. But he is always the first to volunteer to help clean up and do the dishes.

I began to fish with Wally one year in Canada when he filled in at the last minute for another guy, Ricky, who couldn't come on our annual weeklong trip. For several years afterward, I fished with Wally just one week per year. It was a Wednesday, the last week of June 2006, when we headed out one morning for what would become a very memorable day.

We started out that morning on Muskrat Lake, Ontario, about 8:15 AM. Sounds late but we generally fished until dark, and we didn't believe that this Canadian lake required an earlier start. Wally was in my boat; my friend Dave and his father, Bill, Wally's best friend, were in the other boat.

Now Wally had done a lot of fishing in his 75 years. He used to routinely fish tournaments on Lake Chautauqua, New York, for largemouth bass. Today we were after smallmouth bass and pike. I was running the foot-controlled trolling motor from the front of my 17½ foot bass boat. Believe me when I tell you the guy in the front of the boat has all the advantage and can use it if he so chooses.

But if you fish with a person like Wally you want him to be successful. The joy on his face and the "Holy man!" exclamation when he gets a good fish are priceless. So I positioned the boat along the rock wall so Wally could get a good cast.

I continued a similar method of fishing all day, and Wally took advantage of it. He caught one fish after another—big smallmouths—in fact, the biggest of the week. We landed them in the net, snapped a picture, and quickly released the beautiful bronzebacks.

Now I did all right, too. But it quickly became apparent that this would be a special day for Wally, so much so he couldn't wait to get back to the cabin to tell the story of this day to Dave and Bill.

"The best day of fishing in my entire life!" he exclaimed as we sat at the supper table. Each big fish, each hook set or special lure was relived over dinner. And I was being thanked for it.

I remembered that day as I drove to Joanne's funeral the following year, showing up unexpectedly after a five-hour drive to pay my respects. And Wally remembered it, too, in exactly the same way. "The best day of fishing I ever had," he said as he hugged me and thanked me for coming.

What a gift—"the best day of fishing ever"—in 75 years. However, I knew the true gift had been given to me.

Father's Day

The water was exceptional that day—sparkling with an unusual clarity, not much of a chop, and little wind.

It was June, it was the Chesapeake, it was my younger son's first charter fishing trip—it was Father's Day. *It doesn't get any better than this,* I thought at the time.

We were headed out of Kentmoor Marina, Maryland, with one of the premier charter captains in the state—he guides for the governor—on one of the classic of all Chesapeake charter boats, the Breezin' Thru.

Oh, this boat is special for many reasons: Its style—a classic Chesapeake fishing boat, wooden, low and stable in the water. Its heritage since its construction in 1934—only two owners, Captain Harry Carter and Captain Tilghman Hemsley. Its cuisine—at day's end guests are treated to world-class eating. Consider the average fare: fresh striped bass, fresh blue fish, Chesapeake crab cakes, steamed blue claws, spicy Bloody Mary's, and fresh baked chocolate chip cookies.

The Breezin' Thru has a special feel about it. When you get on it, you know right away that it is unique. The woodwork and brass fittings are exceptional. The hardwood floor creaks like an old house as you make your way to the cabin to unload your gear.

The smell is a combination of salt, fish, diesel fuel, and old seasoned wood. It is unusual but comforting. It welcomes you aboard. You sense that this is what Chesapeake fishing should be, and immediately your heart starts beating a little faster in anticipation of the day ahead.

This particular day would indeed be special. Brennan was eleven. He was by nature a restless child—inquisitive, perceptive, and constantly seeking to be active or entertained. Our captain, Tilghman, sensed this and immediately took Brennan aside to get him "locked-in" to his forthcoming Chesapeake adventure.

The boat included a small aquarium that housed a sea turtle. The turtle was hungry; and as we sat in the boat at the dock enjoying our scrambled eggs, bacon, and biscuits, Brennan was permitted to feed the turtle some of his bacon. Of course, this was a hit. Before long, breakfast was being ignored, much to the apparent delight of the terrapin sea creature that got piece after piece of Brennan's bacon.

After breakfast on the dock, we were on our way. The wind was cool as the boat ran smoothly across the bay. We headed down to the flats below Blood Point to set up for the day. The salt air smelled good and Captain Tilghman engaged Brennan in all things nautical: the depth finder, the radio, the radar, the boat controls—it was Seamanship 101, and my son loved it!

I began to relax. I worry more than I should, and on this day my anxiety level was high as I was concerned that my son, who was more into soccer and guitars, would be quickly bored with fishing. But he had settled in nicely and was engaged and anxious to catch his first Chesapeake striper.

The captain positioned the Breezin' Thru among just a few other boats that had reported early success. The sun was just coming up and its glow already warmed our faces and hands. The captain dropped the anchor and the activity level on the boat quickly intensified. The mate, Will, Captain Tilghman's son, reached overhead to get the rods down from their storage. He opened the bait box, rigged the lines, and dipped and threw chum, a smelly mess of ground-up bunker fish, overboard to attract the stripers into our general area.

Each baited hook had either a clam, a bunker chunk, or a bunker heart on it. Brennan was a bit fascinated, and a bit put off by a fish heart that was now impaled on a hook on the end of his line.

The lines floated weightless in the tidal current behind us. We were instructed to leave our bails open until we felt a "difference" on the end of the line, at which time we should close the bail and set the hook. At first, we were unsuccessful at hooking any fish, and our bait was being lost to the hungry but stealthy creatures.

Captain Tilghman took great interest in Brennan's technique. He helped him feed the line out slowly, resting a thumb on the monofilament to detect the slightest strike. Then it happened! A 20" striper inhaled Brennan's bait and the fight was on!

Brennan wound his reel. He wound too fast! He wound too hard! But wind he did and Will skillfully netted the frisky 20" silver-striped beauty. As the fish came over the side of the boat, Brennan's face beamed with pride. It's fun to catch fish. It's even more fun to catch the first fish.

Our cameras flashed, recording the moment. The fish was held long ways, sideways, with and without Dad in the picture, with and without the captain in the picture. Oh, it was fun! A grand moment!

Brennan continued to catch fish the rest of the day. In fact, he became rather skillful at it. No longer requiring the captain's assistance, he would call out as he detected a bite and set the hook. It was a joy to watch, as picture after picture was taken. Each fish seemed a little bigger, or a better fighter, or fatter, or just something to make it noteworthy, and picture worthy as well!

Recipes

You Wanna Great Burger?

Ingredients

Venison burgers, no more than ½" thick
McCormick's Broiled Steak Seasoning
Worcestershire sauce
Butter
Onion slices
Good bread or rolls
Ketchup

Instructions

Make a nice sized burger patty and sprinkle both sides with the seasoning. Melt some butter over medium heat in a good frying pan. Add a few splashes of Worcestershire sauce. When butter is hot (but not burning turning brown), place the thawed burgers in the pan. Cook about two minutes and flip to the other side for about two minutes, then flip again. Don't smash the burgers with the spatula! Wait about one minute and flip again. Watch the heat, don't let them burn. Continue flipping every couple of minutes until the last of the blood stops leaking from the top of the burger. They are ready! Let them rest for a minute. Place on the bread/roll and top with the sliced onions and ketchup. Delicious!

Wally's Pork Chops

Menu
Grilled Pork Chops
Grilled Potato Slices
Green Beans
Sliced Tomatoes
Chocolate Chip Cookies

Ingredients
Center cut pork chops, one or two per person
Extra Virgin Olive Oil (EVOO)
Baked potatoes, one per person
Green Beans (fresh or frozen)
Sliced Tomatoes

Instructions

Lay pork chops on a glass plate. Pierce both sides with a fork several times and sprinkle both sides with salt and pepper. Pour enough EVOO over the chops to barely cover and make sure the EVOO is under the chops as well as over them. If you like extra flavor, you may also add a little dried thyme and rosemary.

While the chops are resting, place the potatoes in the microwave. (If you don't have one, the potatoes need to be baked at 400 degrees for 40 minutes ahead of time.) When potatoes are done, slice them about 1/3 inch thick, skins on. Then brush the slices with EVOO and sprinkle with salt and pepper.

If you have fresh green beans, place them in a shallow pan with just enough water to cover. Put the pan on a low flame and cover. Bring them to a slow simmer and check them for doneness by breaking a bean. Cook until done to taste, drain, and add a little butter and fresh ground pepper. If frozen, follow package directions, adding butter, salt, and pepper when done.

Heat gas grill to medium or charcoal grill until coals are gray. Place chops directly on grill and potato slices on a piece of aluminum foil sprayed with Pam. Grill chops about five minutes on one side, then flip over. Do the same with potato slices.

Slice tomatoes and sprinkle with salt, pepper, and a touch of EVOO.

Serve chops, potatoes, and sliced tomatoes on a platter or buffet style. Place green beans in a bowl. Offer chocolate chip cookies with coffee for dessert.

Crab and Salmon Dip (The Chesapeake meets Alaska!)

Ingredients
12 oz. crabmeat
6 oz. smoked salmon
1 package of cream cheese
¼ cup chopped green onion
¼ tsp salt
½ tsp lemon juice
¼ tsp Worcheshire sauce
Black pepper and some cayenne to taste

Mix ingredients together (may need to soften the cream cheese). Top with a few chopped green onions or parsley. Serve with a good cracker.

Rockfish Bites

Ingredients

2 filets from a small rockfish- skinned and
cut into 2inch squares
1 cup EVOO (Extra Virgin Olive Oil)
1 cup Italian bread crumbs
1 cup milk
Sliced lemon
Tartar or cocktail sauce

Heat oil in skillet. Mix egg and milk. Dip fish
in egg and milk mixture, then in the bread
crumbs. Cook in oil until golden brown. Serve
with lemon slices and sauce of choice. Can be
an appetizer or dinner served with coleslaw.

Chapter 4

Reflections from Alaska

Illuminating your soul—sometimes the farther you are willing to go, the farther you get.

The "Eyes" Have It

The glances were more than momentary; in fact, they were stares as the Fish Man joined the guides and guests for breakfast. He had donned his usual garb—sweat pants topped by cut-off sweat pants and a t-shirt. He joined the catalog-outfitted stereotypical Alaskan guides with a hardy "Good Morning," as he quickly became the center of attention.

The guides around the three tables knew that despite his unorthodox appearance—more like a freshman college basketball player than a premier Alaskan fisherman—no one out-fished the Fish Man. And I was glad that I was with him.

Yeah, the guides were "prettier" than he. Everything they wore was the best quality, and it all matched. But the Fish Man was more than just the best fisherman in the region, he was my friend. That's just the way he was. He knew all

about me, and would routinely ask about my family—Donna and Logan and Brennan. How was Logan doing in college? Or how is Brennan's music coming along? These were typical conversation topics. The discussions were never forced or contrived. Rather, they flowed easily at mealtimes or on the porch of his "fish shack" late in the evening over beer and cigars.

But this morning at the lodge would prove to be different. It was a morning that I will never forget for one specific reason—the fish eyes.

You see, Fish Man has a tradition of taking us fishing for Dolly Varden, essentially an Alaskan trout, on the first day of every trip to bring good luck for the rest of the week. On the morning of our first full day of salmon fishing we eat the Dolly for breakfast—the cook already knows that fish will be part of our breakfast—pan-fried whole to Fish Man's specifications.

This day was no exception. Out came the Dolly Varden on our plates, much to the apparent annoyance and perhaps dismay of the other guests. "I can't believe that you would eat something that is looking at you," one of the ladies with the well-groomed and outfitted guides said.

Without missing a beat, Fish Man responded, "You're kidding! The eyes are one of the best parts of any fish!" Then he proceeded to pluck the pea sized bulb out of its socket and pop it into his mouth.

"Ooooohhh!" she squealed, "I can't believe you're eating that!"

Eat it he did. And then so did we, much to the chagrin of our prim and proper fishing guests.

Needless to say, we had an extremely good week of fishing!

"We See You!"

Those eyes never left us,
They watched every inch,
Even as fork approached,
Not once did they flinch.

The bulb left the socket,
And burst like a grape
As his teeth mashed down
Savoring this seafood crepe.

It was all tongue in cheek,
And, yes, he did know,
That the guided ones fumed
At his commanding this show.

But outfits and gear
Don't mean nothing to "Fish."
We had one hell of a week
As they left with a wish!

Life's Lights

The spirits, voices, and laughter of unborn children—that's what the Aurora Borealis or Northern Lights are according to Native Alaskan legend. And much like children, we learned that they could be unpredictable and prone to not "behaving" and doing what was expected of them. What we expected was that because we were in Alaska and it was dark outside, we would, of course, see this legendary nighttime display every night—easier said than done.

In addition to cloudy, rainy, or overcast evenings, there was also the fact that on any given evening, in fact, more often than not, they just didn't appear. And when you have fished all day, been in the Alaskan air that does in fact "smell" better than any other air I have ever known, and had dinner and drinks, it's hard to do anything other than relax and sleep when it finally gets dark around 10 PM.

But this night was different. We had "limited out" for salmon early this day and were back at the lodge earlier than usual. The dinner of halibut bites and Alaskan salad on our guide Fish Man's deck was over, and the evening seemed young.

"Let's go for a drive and look for some bears up by the lake," Fish Man suggested. We jumped at the chance, grabbing some spotlights and my best 35mm camera. We had not seen a bear this trip so far; in fact, the father-son team that accompanied me had never seen a bear in the wild and were chomping at the bit to do so.

The "Fishmobile," named so as everything associated with Fish Man is "Fish" something or other, creaked and rattled up the old dirt and stone road by Eyak Lake. Without the artificial light we are so accustomed to, it was dark—stretch your hand out in front of you and not be able to see it dark.

It didn't take long until we came upon a pile of still-steaming bear scat in the center of the road—a good sign! Close by was the bleeding carcass of a freshly killed salmon. Did the van scare the bear away? Probably, we surmised. We flooded the dense brush with our spotlights to no avail.

The thought of being in this dark place without the van, without the Fish Man was, well, terrifying to me. It was scary enough as it was. We didn't talk, we listened. We listened to nothing—absolutely pure unadulterated silence. And we could see nothing but the Alaskan blackness.

That is until it started to happen—the Alaskan lights.

They were not what I had expected. In my mind's eye, they would be rays of red and yellow shooting out from the earth. Instead, it was much more like a chartreuse nighttime rainbow that arced over the lake, high in the sky and then slowly descended to earth.

That's when Fish Man told us of the legend. He said, "You're watching the spirits of unborn children." Wow! I knew that what we were beholding was heaven-sent, but this ancient legend just shared with us made the event even more miraculous for me. No cause-and-effect explanation could ever allow me to rationalize what I was seeing into strict scientific terms. It was a miracle—another vivid demonstration of God's handiwork that seems so easy to find in so many places in Alaska.

I put my camera on the rooftop of the Fishmobile to steady it and set the exposure at the slowest aperture rate that I had, hoping in some way to catch the beauty on film. The bear by now had been forgotten. Instead, the four of us stood so silently the click of the shutter when it finally closed almost startled us. Not even the jokester dad interfered with the moment by yelling, "Bear!" or emitting any residual noise left over from dinner.

It was pure peace that could not, or would not, ever be duplicated in my life again. I was mesmerized. I was numb. I was speechless. I was in awe. I had a moment of moments, one that put every bit of trouble or unrest that I had ever had in my life at rest, normalized, and in perspective.

We drove back to the lodge, only the rattling Fishmobile unable or unwilling to be silent. That night, I had one of the most restful, deep sleep nights of my life.

Run Dick, Run!

We haven't seen that many bears in Alaska. But we have seen enough to be leery of them while fishing along the deserted streams and rivers that we love to explore and fish. However, we were unaware of the bear that was shot and killed a mile or so above us as we fished Clear Creek in September 2005.

We didn't know that anything special had happened that day until we returned to Rose Lodge where we were staying. There was a "buzz" about the place regarding the huge bear that was taken that day on the creek. In fact, some had seen it in town at the hunter's house. It didn't take long for us to get there.

The bear was enormous! It was over 9' tall and one of its paws almost covered the chest of the 6'4" young man who worked for CNBC as he displayed it for us. The teeth were

long and yellow, and it had an odor about it that I had heard of and until now had thought was exaggerated.

The butchering had already started and the meat would be frozen, brined, smoked, or canned, or some combination of those processes. CNBC guy—I have forgotten his name—told us he shot the bear in self-defense. He was canoeing above us as we fished when the bear came to the creek's bank, no more than 15' from him. CNBC guy had a license and a gun, but he preferred not to take his bear that way. We later learned, and saw vivid photos of his previous takes using either a bow and arrow or even a spear. Yes, we thought he was a little crazy, too! In any event, feeling threatened because one leap and the bear would be on him, he fired two shots to kill his perceived opponent.

The father and son team on this trip had been urging Fish Man all day to take us out to see the bears "up close and personal"—they now had a different outlook on things.

"Man, I never want to see one of those while I'm fishing," exclaimed the son.

"Me either," Dad chimed in.

I had to throw in my two cents worth, "My view hasn't changed, and I'm not concerned."

"You've got to be kidding!" said Dad who was in his 50s and somewhat portly. "You don't think you can outrun something like that, do you?" he challenged.

"No," I said, "but I can outrun you...and that's all that matters."

Enough said!

The "Eck"

Fish Man carried a gun when we went into bear country, especially brown bear country. He would remain on post with the dull black weapon laid across his lap while we fished. His eyes scanning the landscape for a bush that moved, his ears tuned

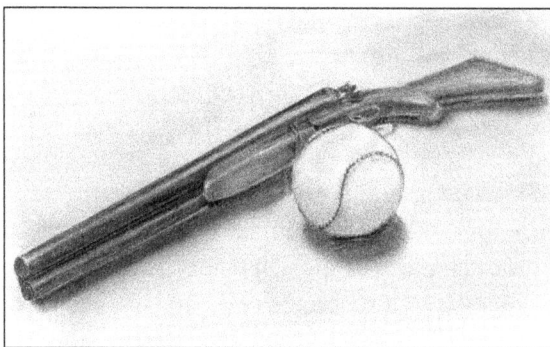

to the crack of a twig, and his nose sniffing for a whiff of that unmistakable stink of a bear.

Now, Fish Man generally would cast a lure or a fly with us as we fished, but not in bear country. The extra rod stayed in the Fishmobile, and the gun that he referred to as the "Eck" would stay firmly planted in his hands instead. The Eck was essentially a short-barreled 12-gauge shotgun loaded with high power bear slug shells. It was serious business!

As far as the name Eck, I asked Fish Man about it. Bear in mind, no pun intended, that Fish Man has a name for everything. There's the Fishmobile, Alaska Fishmobile, the Fish Shack, and Fish Storage, to name a few, but the Eck comes from his other passion, baseball.

In the 1970s and '80s, the Oakland A's had a pitcher named Dennis Eckersley, a great pitcher who went on to become one of the game's greatest closers. As Fish Man tells it, when the Eck came out, the game was over. So, too, it was with his gun. If the Eck is used, "The game is over, one way or another!"

All I can say is, "I'm rooting for the home team!"

Smoked King Collar

If you ever get the opportunity to try something called a "smoked king collar," take advantage of it. The King Salmon is by far the largest salmon, sometimes weighing up to 80 pounds. The "collar" is a piece of the fish that is generally "discarded" at most commercial fish processing plants. I put "discarded" in quotation marks because even though it is almost always removed, it is very rarely thrown away even though it never makes its way to retail fish outlets.

The collar is the piece of the King Salmon behind the head and just in front of the adipose fin. It might be 1-1½" thick, and it resembles a fish horseshoe with wings (fins). It contains some of the finest and most richly omega 3 oil-saturated pieces of salmon available.

The locals compete to have this prize once removed, and all kinds of local fare are made from it. The most famous method of preparing it, however, is to slowly smoke it over alder wood and then consume it once finished.

The meat is distinctly different from the rest of the salmon. It is almost stringy in texture and darker. Have you ever found that spoon-size piece of meat on the Thanksgiving turkey that

rests in the long cavity at the rear of the backbone when cleaning it for soup? It's like that!

Fish Man got us some king collar one night as appetizers, and to quote the judge who was fishing with us—well, it was almost orgasmic.

Just eat it with your fingers and some crackers and a cold beer.

I actually have a source to mail order occasionally the very best of Alaskan King Salmon collars. If you are interested, email me for details.

Good-bye Gaye

Gaye McDowell ran the Rose Lodge. Her responsibilities were immense. Imagine going grocery shopping every other week and having the task consume 48 hours of time. The trip to the "store" included taking the van on the ferry to Valdez and then to Anchorage, a 10-hour trip, and shopping and loading the van with over $5,000 worth of groceries, then making the return ferry ride home. This was just a minor part of Gaye's routine chores.

She managed the reservations, scheduled the fishing trips, cooked, cleaned, and hired and trained all the help. Gary, her husband, was an active partner. He routinely guided the fishing excursions on the Eyak, cleaned and vacuum-packed the fresh salmon, and helped in the kitchen. But Gary would be the first to tell you that Gaye was the "Boss." And we knew it, too.

As Jim Croce sang, "You don't tug on Superman's cape," and you didn't mess with Gaye. She was as tough as they came.

When she told you to do something, or scolded you, her voice, gravelly from years of smoking combined with her Georgia accent, left absolutely no doubt that you had but one choice, "Listen up!" Like being at breakfast on time. If you signed up to eat at 7 AM, your fully prepared breakfast was on the table at 7 AM whether you were at the table or not.

Gaye did well in this modern-day Alaskan outpost, just as she would have 100 years ago in some Western frontier town. She was a survivor; she meant business, and she knew what it took to run a lodge full of sometimes less than cooperative fishermen.

The last time I saw Gaye, she wasn't feeling well. She had cancer, but was hopeful of recovery. You wouldn't have known anything was wrong to see her or to talk to her. She was strong; and, in fact, doing well with the treatments and the surgery

except for one thing—an infection, perhaps a staph infection. Either it or the medication she was taking was making her groggy and faint. So much so, that it was decided to take her by helicopter to the Anchorage Hospital shortly before Christmas 2007.

Gary said good-bye to his wife on that December day as the medevac helicopter, the pilot, and the two medical technicians left Cordova. It was only 40 minutes later the chopper went down in the Prince William Sound. One body, not Gaye's, and a helicopter door were the only remnants of the wreckage to be found.

Gaye's body never was recovered, and Gary went on to run the lodge without her. We pray for them both. They were a couple destined to be together—and to this day, we miss the thorny flower from the Cordova Rose Lodge.

Recipes

Northern Lights Meal

Menu

Halibut Bites with Dipping Sauce
Alaskan Salad
Crusty French Rolls with Butter and a
Good Jelly (Fireweed Jelly if possible)

Ingredients

Fresh halibut
1 egg
½ cup milk

Reflections from Alaska

Italian Seasoned Bread Crumbs
6 tablespoons butter
French rolls
Tartar or cocktail sauce
Mix of iceberg lettuce and spinach
Ripe tomatoes cut into chunks
Raspberry vinaigrette
Cold, cooked Alaskan King Crab

Instructions

Cut halibut into large, bite-size chunks, about 2" x 2". Beat egg and mix with milk. Dip halibut chunks in egg/milk mixture and roll into seasoned bread crumbs. Let the chunks rest while you melt butter in a non-stick skillet. When the butter is bubbly but not brown, put the halibut chunks in the pan and monitor; turn until golden brown on all sides.

Serve with heated French rolls (450 degrees for 5-6 minutes) and salad made from last four ingredients.

You can buy good tartar sauces, Bookbinder's is quality, or make your own with mayonnaise, chopped pickles, and a little Worcestershire sauce. Catsup mixed with horseradish or store-bought cocktail sauce is a favorite of many with this fish. Try some Alaskan Pale Ale with this meal if you can get it.

Cordova Rose Lodge Breakfast

Menu

Gaye's French Toast
Reindeer Sausage
Scrambled Eggs with Old Bay
Blueberry Muffins

Ingredients: French Toast

4 eggs
1 cup milk
½ teaspoon vanilla
8 slices day-old bread (may use French
bread or good homemade bread,
store-bought will do)
4 tablespoons butter
Powdered sugar

Instructions: French Toast

Beat the eggs, milk, and vanilla together until frothy. Dip the bread slices into the mixture and fry on a hot griddle in melted butter until golden brown. Serve sprinkled with powdered sugar.

Ingredients: Scrambled Eggs

8 eggs
Old Bay Seasoning
2 tablespoons butter

Instructions: Scrambled Eggs

Beat the eggs until frothy. Melt the butter in a skillet set to medium high heat. Pour the eggs into the heated skillet onto the melted butter. Lift and stir the egg mixture gently allowing it to set up a bit but not turn solid. As the eggs cook, sprinkle them with ground black pepper and Old Bay seasoning to color. Serve slightly moist.

Easy Fancy Grilled Salmon

Ingredients

1 two-pound salmon filet
½ cup mayonnaise
1 teaspoon mustard
½ cup chopped green onion
Splash of Worcestershire sauce
1/8 teaspoon garlic salt
1/8 teaspoon salt
¼ teaspoon pepper
1 bunch of Romaine lettuce
Fresh tomatoes
Italian dressing

Instructions

Mix together mayo, mustard, onions, and Worcestershire sauce. Place mixture in refrigerator. Spray a grill or fish holder with Pam. Place filet, skin side up, on the hot surface and cook for 5-6 minutes. Flip over and cover with refrigerated spice mixture. Salt and pepper to taste. Grill over medium heat for 10-12 minutes or until flakes easily.

Split a head of Romaine lettuce and brush with EVOO. Salt and pepper to taste. Place on grill with salmon for last 5-6 minutes, flipping once.

Slice fresh tomatoes, sprinkle with Italian dressing.

A Baseball Kind of Meal

Ingredients

Kielbasa—moose, caribou, or something
store-bought
Sliced onions and green peppers
Dijon or other hot mustard
Oversized rolls—hoagie or French-style bread
Crunchy pickles like Clausen
Lard-cooked potato chips (for example, Gibbles
http://www.potatoroll.com/pages/snacks.asp)

Instructions

Sauté together onions and peppers on the grill on a griddle. At the same time, grill the kielbasa, don't overcook it.

Serve on roll with pickles, chips, and lots of hot mustard.

This is a great meal to cook by the river with a fresh piece of fish. I like seasoned salmon!

Fish Man Rollups

Ingredients

Smoked salmon
4 ounces of cream cheese, softened
to room temperature
1 cup of salsa
Tortilla

Instructions

Blend salmon with cream cheese into paste. Add salt and pepper to taste. Spread the paste on a tortilla and cover with salsa. Roll up and slice with dental floss. Serve cold.

For a hot dish, top roll ups with crabmeat and shredded cheddar cheese. Bake at 325 degrees for 25 minutes. Serve hot right out of the oven!

Good-for-Once Salmon Cakes

Menu

GFO Salmon Cakes
Sliced Tomatoes
Buttered Noodles
Sliced Canned Pears

Ingredients

¼ teaspoon each salt and pepper
Old Bay Seasoning
Touch of red pepper
½ tablespoon chopped green onion
½ teaspoon horseradish
½ teaspoon lemon juice
1 pound cooked salmon
1 beaten egg
½ cup of bread crumbs (Panko crumbs
quite good)
Extra Virgin Olive Oil (EVOO)
Fresh tomatoes
Bag of egg noodles
Can of sliced pears

Instructions

If salmon is frozen, you can microwave it in a freezer bag with holes pricked in the top. Cook 4 minutes on defrost until cooked but still moist. Mix first seven ingredients except for egg and bread crumbs. Shape mixture into four cakes, dip in beaten egg and roll in bread crumbs. Refrigerate for one hour.

Heat EVOO in non-stick fry pan until shimmering then add cakes and fry until golden brown, then turn them over and continue frying until golden all over. Serve at once with cocktail sauce, tartar sauce, or remoulade sauce. Add a slice of tomato, purple onion, and/or Romaine lettuce if you like.

Serve with warm buttered noodles, sliced tomatoes, and sliced canned pears.

Salmon Salad

Ingredients

Salmon filet

½ fresh orange

Sesame seeds

½ small can of Mandarin oranges

Shredded Romaine lettuce

Extra Virgin Olive Oil (EVOO)

Balsamic vinegar

Soy sauce

Fresh tomatoes, regular or cherry

Can of LaChoy Chow Mein noodles

Salt and pepper

Bag of Pepperidge Farm French Rolls

Instructions

Onto the thawed salmon filet, squeeze the juice of the ½ fresh orange and sprinkle with soy sauce. Heat a frying pan to medium high and add some EVOO to cover the bottom. Coat the salmon with sesame seeds and sauté about 4 minutes per side.

Follow the directions on the bag to heat the rolls.

To assemble the salad, place some shredded Romaine lettuce on a dinner plate. Mix EVOO and balsamic vinegar or use bottled balsamic vinaigrette. Place the salmon on the lettuce, and surround it with the fresh tomato slices or cherry tomatoes. Top with the dressing, salt and pepper, and sprinkle the crispy noodles on the salad.

Serve with crusty, hot rolls and enjoy!

Tangy Salmon

Ingredients

1 pound salmon filet, skinned
¼ cup melted butter

Reflections from Alaska

¼ cup Extra Virgin Olive Oil (EVOO)
1 tablespoon lemon juice
1/8 teaspoon minced garlic
¼ teaspoon salt
¼ teaspoon pepper

Instructions

Mix all the ingredients except the salmon in a small bowl.

Using a sharp knife, remove the salmon skin and discard.

Place the salmon on a large platter or in a large glass baking pan and pour the butter mixture over it. Cover and place in the refrigerator for at least 30 minutes.

Prepare a charcoal grill or preheat a gas grill to medium. Spray a cooking basket with vegetable or grill spray and place the salmon in the basket. Brush the leftover marinade on the salmon and grill it about 10 minutes per inch of thickness, turning once.

I like this meal served with fresh, steamed Brussels sprouts with lots of butter and a good, cold, chunky applesauce.

Salmon with Spinach and Shrimp

You will need three frying pans for the recipe, but it's terrific, looks elegant, and easy to prepare.

Ingredients

1 pound skinless salmon filet
1 cup fresh shrimp (16 ct or smaller)
Good handful of baby spinach
1 green onion (chopped)
½ cup white wine
1 tablespoon butter
1 tablespoon flour
½ cup milk
chives
1/3 teaspoon chopped garlic
Salt and pepper
Extra Virgin Olive Oil (EVOO)

Sauté spinach after heating pan with EVOO and garlic. Reduce and hold on warm. Begin sauce by sautéing onion in butter—add wine, butter, flour, and milk; keep stirring. Add shrimp when salmon is almost done. Cook 1-2 minutes till pink. At the same time, salt and pepper filet and sauté in EVOO; cook approximately 3-4 minutes per side.

To serve, place spinach on plate, top with salmon. Pour sauce with shrimp onto salmon. Sprinkle with chives.

Brine for Smoked Salmon

Ingredients

1 cup Kosher salt
¼ cup brown sugar
Fresh ground black pepper
Chopped garlic
Lemon juice
10 cups water

Instructions

Mix all together in a large soup kettle. Brine salmon according to the instructions in your smoker manual.

Salmon Primer

Alaskan Salmon Types

There are five types of salmon found in Alaskan waters:

Type*	Protein	Fat Content	Calories	Season	Remarks
Sockeye (Red)	36g	15g	286	May-Sept	High oil content, deep red color. The second most abundant species after Pink. Do not overcook any salmon, especially this one. Great for canning, broiling, or grilled.

Coho (Silver)	37g	10g	248	July-Sept	My personal favorite, orange/red firm flesh. A King lookalike, only smaller. Delicate flavor, the most versatile salmon in terms of preparation. Good for grilling, broiling, or baking.
King (Chinook)	34g	18g	304	June-Aug	The most expensive salmon with the highest oil content and richest flavor. Bright red flesh. The "filet mignon" of the ocean. The largest of the salmon family. Good for baking, broiling, or grilling.
Pink (Humpy, hump-back)	34g	6g	197	July-Aug	The most abundant species. Pink flesh with a texture similar to a trout. Lower fat and mild. Good for grilling but mostly canned. Try it for salmon cakes.
Chum (Dog or Keta), also Silver-bright.	34g	6g	204	June-Oct	Pink flesh, lower oil content and firm texture. This and Pink are the least expensive. Good for smoking. Or cooking as you would a mild white fish

*Based on a 6 oz. serving.

By comparison, a 6 oz. serving of farm-raised Atlantic salmon has 34 grams of protein, 19 grams of fat, and 311 calories. For a variety of reasons I am not a fan of Atlantic farm raised salmon.

Salmon—Know What You Are Buying

Read the labels before you purchase salmon. Look for salmon labeled "wild caught" or better still "Line caught wild salmon." In Alaska, all salmon are wild; in fact, it is illegal to farm-raise salmon in Alaska.

You may see fish labeled "Pacific Salmon." That does not mean that it is wild as there are farm-raised Pacific salmon coming in from Canada and Chile.

Atlantic salmon are farm-raised, all of them. They are from a different family or species of salmon and do not have the same flavor or texture as "wild" Alaskan salmon.

Look for:

- Fish that have a good ocean aroma. Fish should not smell bad or have an ammonia smell.
- The flesh should be firm and not dried out.
- The eyes should be bright; the skin should be shiny.

For more information, visit www.pssifish.com.

My Wish for You

I hope you have enjoyed this trip down my memory lane—enough so that you will start writing your own views of life from your own special place(s). Give your family and friends something to ponder, to laugh about, to shake their heads and smirk about—and give yourself permission to relax and recall all the wild and wooly, calm and content, exciting and exhilarating times during your life's journey in the great outdoors.

My Outdoor Journal

Making Your Life in the Outdoors

My Outdoor Journal

Making Your Life in the Outdoors

My Outdoor Journal

Making Your Life in the Outdoors

My Outdoor Journal

Making Your Life in the Outdoors

About the Author

Warren grew up in south central Pennsylvania. Born in the 1950's he lost his father at the age of 5. In a family of two older sisters and a mother that often worked two jobs Warren was left to his own devices in terms of growing up. The family lived close to the Yellow Breeches Creek, and it was there that Warren taught himself to fish.

His cooking skills came out of necessity. Both his sisters were soon out of the house, and with his mother working evenings, it became clear that there was little other choice. He found that he enjoyed cooking and as he grew older he got more creative. But he has always enjoyed cooking game and fish the most.

Warren has hunted at the same cabin, in the same spot since 1983- Archie's Cabin. Warren loves Archies, named after the founder and builder of the cabin, Archie Strickland. The modest cabin has 125 windows! They are former jewelery case glass bought from an old department store. Archie was thrifty to a fault. But it is a good place, and after Archie died in 2000 Warren bought the property from his son Tony.

Warren had a very successful political career but walked away from it at the peak of his popularity because he wanted to protect our natural resources, particularly water. He volunteered with the PA Fish and Boat Commission and the Chesapeake Bay Commission. He was appointed by the US Secretary of Commerce as a member of the Mid-Atlantic Fishery Management Council, where he oversees the Ocean Planning and Ecosystem Committee.

Warren wrote this book in the hope that others will learn to appreciate our natural resources and how important it is for us to find our place in the "natural world".

www.ingramcontent.com/pod-product-compliance
Lightning Source LLC
Chambersburg PA
CBHW062002040426
42447CB00010B/1862